BE STILL

Inspired Writings
By
Sandra J Yearman

Seraphim Publishing LLC

WE WILL BRING LIGHT TO ALL THE DARK PLACES

Registered trademark-Sandra J Yearman
Seraphim Publishing
438 Water St
Cambridge, WI 53523

Copyright © 2008 Sandra J Yearman
Produced in the United States of America
Author : Sandra J Yearman
Editor: Sandra J Yearman
Cover Design by Sandra J Yearman
Layout and design by Sandra J Yearman

All rights reserved. No part of this book may be reproduced, stored in or introduced into a retrieval system, or transmitted, in any form or by any means, electronic or mechanical, including photocopying or recording or otherwise copied for public or private use—other than for "fair use" as brief quotations embodied in articles and reviews—without written permission from the author.

Library of Congress Control Number: 2009912319
ISBN: 978-0-9841506-3-2
First Edition

Be Still And Know I AM God
For I Will Make A Way
And Rescue All My Children
Even In The Darkest Days
Amen
Amen
Amen

CONTENTS

DEDICATION

Be Still..7
The Lamb Who Sacrificed.............................9
Riches Unseen.......................................11
Precious Is His Name................................14
The Promise..17
In The Stillness.....................................19
New Year...20
Glory And The Dove..................................22
The Walk He Took Alone..............................24
My Purpose..26
He Carried And He Blessed..........................28
I Promise To Dance..................................30

SEEKING LIGHT IN THE DARKNESS

Disposable Lives....................................33
Flag Draped Coffins.................................35
Each Heart..38
Disillusioned.......................................40
My Voice..42

CONTENTS

Spirit Of The Lord.................................45
Hiding In The Darkness........................48
The Blessing And The Curse................50
Crown Of Thorns..................................52
Battle Songs Lose Their Meaning........54
In The Eyes Of A Child........................56
Snow Flakes...58
I Heard A Song.....................................60
He Called Into The Darkness...............62
That We May Realize............................65

COMING HOME

Always...68
Faith Is The Answer..............................70
Call To Worship....................................72
The Eastern Light Did Raise................74
You Are Not Alone...............................76
His Footsteps Are Before Us................77
Shelter Beneath His Wings..................79

Dedication

Be Still

Be still and know I AM God
For I will make a Way
And rescue all My children
Even in the darkest days

Be still and know I AM God
My Promises to keep
I will carry your burdens
I will dry your tears, when you weep

Be still and know I AM God
Blessings I do give
For all who believe
Eternal Life to Live

Be still and know I AM God
These words for you are meant
The Love of Heaven Lives
Through the Son to you, I sent

Amen Amen Amen

The Lamb Who Sacrificed

They stood before the opening
Of a tomb that could not contain our Lord
A Miracle most extraordinary
Justice and the Sword

An act that would change time
And the course of this known world
A Covenant given
The Angels did herald

Mankind was changed forever
With the Promise, Heaven sent
To know the Love of a Father
And the Blessings of Heaven as they were meant

Glory be to Jesus
The Lamb who sacrificed
The Father who fought darkness
The Light dissolved the night

Amen Amen Amen

Riches Unseen

God help me to see through
The darkness of this world

Help me to hear
Your Voice in the chaos

Help me to learn
The language of Heaven

So that darkness
No longer consumes my tongue

And never let me forget
That I am blessed

I am blessed through
The trials and tests

I am blessed through
The challenges and joy

I am blessed through
My very existence

I am blessed because
I can be tested

I am blessed because
You are with me through the trials

I am blessed because
Whether I conquer or fall, You will hold me

I am truly blessed

Amen Amen Amen

Precious Is His Name

Glory Alleluia
Precious is His Name
The Father and the Savior
The Holy Lamb who came

To protect us in these dark worlds
Our disfigurements to heal
To save us from ourselves
In praise we do kneel

Glory Alleluia
Precious is our King
Glory Alleluia
Through eternity to ring

Blessed be His Name always
Our Father One in Three
Holy be His Honor
Jesus sent from Thee

Glory Alleluia
Precious be His Name
The Blessings of the Father
The Love of the Same

Glory Alleluia
Glory in His Right
Glory Alleluia
The Light dissolved the night

Alleluia
Alleluia
Alleluia

Amen Amen Amen

The Promise

I will protect you always
Is a promise that I made
To the tortured and the neglected
To the wounded and the slain

I will stand before your darkness
I will take your pain
I will pray to My Father
Your very souls to gain

Always and forever
Is the promise that I make
I was sent to teach you
Deliverance from hate

And through all eternities
The ages do not change
The Promise sent from Heaven
Lives to rearrange

Amen Amen Amen

In The Stillness

In the stillness of our minds, God
speaks to us
Our hearts hear the Holy Song
Our souls weave God's tapestry
For Heaven we do long

In the stillness of our minds
God's Voice is heard, it is true
He calls to us
A Voice that we once knew

Listen very closely
You will hear Him with your heart
A Melody so perfect
A Presence never to part

Amen Amen Amen

New Year

As the clock stuck midnight
Another year had passed
Our future before us
What kind of future, I asked

I bowed my head
On bended knee did pray
God thank You for watching over us
May Your Presence stay

God with this new year
Let not the sign of a horse or water bearer be
Instead oh Lord
Let this year be the sign of Thee

Walk among us in these dark worlds
Change the Course of time and space
Let the Brilliance of Heaven
Bring Light to this dark place

Take an active role in our world
Do not let them shut you out
Do not let the demons drown the voices
Of the victims as they shout

Talk to us as Your children
Help us to see our paths
Help us to conquer the darkness
Help us to do as You asked

Remind us where we came from
That we can conquer the tests
Walk with us always
Let us be the blessed

Amen Amen Amen

Glory And The Dove

Glory and the dove
Blessings from above

Glory be Thy Name
Blessings of the same

The Power of God be known
The Love of God be shown

Glory and the dove
Blessings from above

Eternal is Thy Being
Always is Thy seeing

Bless us with Your Presence here
Always keep Your children near

Glory and the dove
Blessings from above

Amen Amen Amen

The Walk He Took Alone

They threw the palms before Him
The walk He took alone
A mission most Holy
Through Grace our lives Atoned

Our Father, Son and Spirit
The Three and yet the One
Blessed us greatly
Through the Holy Son

The Angels herald the triumph
The Angels sang the Song
The Son from Heaven sent
To cleanse us from our wrong

The palms they threw before Him
The walk He took alone
The Eternal Light from Heaven
The brilliance that was shown

The Love of the Father
The Mercy of the Son
The Grace of the Spirit
Our Lord God Three in One

Amen Amen Amen

My Purpose

What is my purpose
Why am I here
Man asks the questions
But it is the answers they fear

Is there more than this existence
Is there more to these lives
Is there more
Than what we can see with our eyes

What are our boundaries
My choices, I am told
Questions of the sages
Questions of old

Does God define me
Or is it my fear
What if I want to break through my prison
And call the Heavens near

The answers are before us
They are in God's Song
Simply call out His Name
Ask to correct what is wrong

Amen Amen Amen

He Carried And He Blessed

He carried our crosses in battle
Pain only He could endure
The Loving Father before us
A Home in Heaven to ensure

He bore the weight of our deeds
On shoulders held by our Lord
Because of the Grace of Heaven
There was Justice and the Sword

He forgave the darkness in all His children
No matter their wants and deeds
The Blessings of the Spirit
The Love of One in Three

He showed us Miracles
Our Faith He did test
He lit the Path to Heaven
He carried and He Blessed

Amen Amen Amen

I Promise To Dance

Lord let me hear the Song of Heaven
A sound so sweet and true
The music of the ages
A Song to Honor You

Lord fill me with the melody
That with Holiness I lift
My life above the darkness
The horror and the rift

Lord let this Song consume me
Let me dance with Holy glee
Let me sing the Song of Heaven
A Song to Honor Thee

And let me never forget the words
Nor forget how to dance
Let my soul sing throughout the ages
This Holy Song of thanks

Amen Amen Amen

Seeking Light In The Darkness

Disposable Lives

Disposable lives
Cries in the dark
Lost and ignored
Bound and apart

Disposable lives
Horror endured
The victims of man
Abused and unheard

Are we blinded
By fear and greed
Too busy to care
To address the needs

Of creation around us
Of life as we were told
No honor, no love
The victims are sold

For the price of our darkness
Our insatiable needs
God please forgive us
And destroy these unholy seeds

God stand before the victims
And restore our Grace
To conquer the darkness
To bring sanity to this place

There is value in life
God created all creatures
Is the tribute to man
To destroy the future

Amen Amen Amen

Flag Draped Coffins

The sky was torn by thunder
The mortars power known
The darkness ripped and shattered
Man's mark again was sown

Rain can not wash away the horror
That man can do to man
Lord stand before our soldiers
Lord take a Holy stand

He was someone's father
She a daughter known
A brother, son and mother
A sister in her own

Rain can not wash away the horror
That man can do to man
Lord stand before our soldiers
Lord take a Holy stand

Flags drape the coffins
Of the warriors sacrifice
The brave men and women
Who gave to protect the rights

Rain can not wash away the horror
That man can do to man
Lord stand before our soldiers
Lord take a Holy stand

Lord engulf them with Your Holiness
Protect them with Your Grace
Lift them up from the darkness
From the God forsaken place

Let Your Angels walk among them
Let it be Your Voice that they hear
In the darkness of the trenches
Always hold them near

Amen Amen Amen

Each Heart

The demons are loose in the world
tonight
Their destruction to all is known
God Bless us with Your Presence
God stand before Your own

In this world of darkness
The horror we decree
God show us Your Mercy
And remind us all of Thee

Send Your Light to guide us
Your Angels, Song to sing
Protect us from the horror
That this earthly existence brings

Let us never waiver
In our Holy Faith
The demons will never conquer
The children blessed by Grace

Help Your children to understand
That Your Presence is here
Each heart simply has to utter
Your Name
To call Your Holiness near

Amen Amen Amen

Disillusioned

He expected them to worship
He expected them to pray
He expected them to seek the Light
That brings darkness into Day

The teacher was disillusioned
By the darkness of the flock
Who said they wanted God
Yet all Holiness did mock

And when they tried to stone him
Others did flee
He fell upon his knees
And cried out to Thee

'Lord save them from their darkness'
'Their hatred and their greed'
'Fill them with the Divine'
'Plant the Holy Seed'

He prayed until the Heavens
Stood before mankind
He asked God to send him
Some sort of Holy sign

And enter into darkness
A Light which shone so bright
It dissolved the monsters
That terrorized the night

Amen Amen Amen

My Voice

I found my voice
Amidst the ashes
The turbulence, the horror
The whips drawn lashes

Alleluia, Alleluia
Alleluia, Alleluia
Alleluia

I saw my soul
In darkness quake
I prayed to God
For Heaven's sake

Alleluia, Alleluia
Alleluia, Alleluia
Alleluia

In my imperfection
I did speak
God Your Holy Path
I do seek

Alleluia, Alleluia
Alleluia, Alleluia
Alleluia

When you pray
God does respond
He answers all
The Holy One

Alleluia, Alleluia
Alleluia, Alleluia
Alleluia

I heard my voice
From darkness cry
I sought the Light
My soul did fly

Alleluia, Alleluia
Alleluia, Alleluia
Alleluia

Until the end of days
Of time
My soul will sing
The bells will chime

Alleluia, Alleluia
Alleluia, Alleluia
Alleluia

Amen Amen Amen

Spirit Of The Lord

May the Spirit of the Lord
Fill the streets
The homes
The hearts of all creation tonight

For I hear the sounds of violence
The voices of the dead
The chaos in the city
Where are God's children led

What is this need for darkness
Pain and pain again
War around us every where
The victims and the slain

May the Spirit of the Lord
Fill the streets
The homes
The hearts of all creation tonight

For I see the littered bodies
The victories of death
The victims without voices
The walking without breath

What is man's need for destruction
To darken the Light that God sent here
God, hear the voice of Your child
Please bring Your Presence near

May the Spirit of the Lord
Fill the streets
The homes
The hearts of all creation tonight

Amen Amen Amen

Hiding In Darkness

For those who anguish
Of deeds they have done
Victories lost
Songs never sung

For those who dwell in darkness
Afraid to expose
The guilt and the shame
The paths that they chose

For those who are gnarled
And disfigured by hate
Crippled by fear
For death do they wait

The choice is still yours
Call out His Name
Ask for forgiveness
And Blessings of the same

Hope never leaves you
It is you who dim the light
Call out His Name
Ask Him to save you from the night

Amen Amen Amen

The Blessing And The Curse

The Holy choice of Heaven
The Blessing and the curse
Do we choose to walk with man
Or for God's Will to thirst

Can we see through the illusions
Do our senses tell us what is real
Do we glorify our frailties
Or to the Heavens kneel

Man binds himself with boundaries
To justify his fear
His guilt is ever present
His darkness ever near

Yet do we condemn ourselves
By the choices that we make
Then let me cry to Heaven
The boundaries, I choose to break

Amen Amen Amen

Crown of Thorns

He suffered for our darkness
Our sentences He took
Until that Easter morning
When His resurrection shook

The way we looked at this world
The wonder of what He said
The Promise of a God
Who would raise us from the dead

That morning changed our existence
Our realities and more
The Promise of a God
Whose Love would have us soar

Illusions that were broken
Promises were kept
The Love of a God
A human world that wept

He suffered for our darkness
He took our pain
He was sacrificed
That Heaven we may gain

Amen Amen Amen

Battle Songs Lose Their Meaning

The demons stalked them
And took their lives
They put them in cages
They burnt their wives

The world stood by in horror
Frozen in their fear
Afraid to stand up to the demons
Afraid to call attention near

Battle songs lose their meaning
When all the voices are dead
Who is left to stand
When the world to darkness weds

How can you stand for freedom
When you are shackled to the dark gate
How can you stand for God
When you allow a world of horror and hate

God forgive us
Help us to conquer our fears
Consume us with Your Light
Send Your Angels here

Dissolve the hate and horror
The terror and the greed
Save Your holy children
Give them what they need

Amen Amen Amen

In The Eyes Of A Child

Horror in a child's eyes
Will we ever learn
To let go of the darkness
And to our God to turn

When the screams are so muffled
Because of the chaos in the night
That we can not find the victims
Buried and hiding with fright

When the bodies are so numbered
That the identities are lost
What is the role of man
In the sea that we are tossed

God help us to rise above
The darkness we have made
Send Your Angels to our world
To give us Holy aide

Help us to stop the night
To stand and to say 'no'
We can conquer the darkness
As Jesus' life did show

Amen Amen Amen

Snow Flakes

Take the time to notice
The faces lost in the crowds
The silent screams
Their pain is so loud

Lost and nameless
In a sea of anonymity
Why do we not hear them
Why do we not see

Drowning in darkness
The anguish that they bear
To fear you are invisible
To fear that no one cares

God Bless Your children
And touch them with Your Grace
Let them know forever
They are loved in this place

As original as snow flakes
God created all
Give Him your hand
Answer His call

Amen Amen Amen

I Heard A Song

I heard a song about horror
About darkness unveiled
About victims and their families
About demons that were hailed

As I told this story
To a friend who I hold dear
He showed me other instances
Of the same darkness that is here

In my human condition
I felt anger and felt grief
How could we be such monsters
I was in disbelief

God created us as holy
What satisfies our needs
Why do we call to darkness
And commit horrific deeds

What is the human flaw
What is the test to bear
Can we not rise above the darkness
To God our allegiance swear

God of Love and Mercy
Help Your children to be free
Of the darkness that they call to
Return us all to Thee

Amen Amen Amen

He Called Into The Darkness

I was broken and battered
From the darkness that I bear
I had lost the image of myself
My heart knew only despair

I wandered through the dark roads
I stumbled when I tried to climb
And then in my death
I heard the Voices chime

I realized God had heard me
The prayers that my soul said
That He would help to raise me
I would no longer number among the dead

He showed me an illusion
His Voice my heart did hear
He said, 'My child, I did not leave you'
'I have always been near'

'The darkness you put between us'
'Made me seem far away'
'I have never left you'
'It was you who chose to stray'

He called me from the darkness
My eyes could barely see
I felt the changes in me
A calm came over me

In prayer there is power
Through prayer there is the Way
Through prayer my essence returned to me
The night has turned to day

Amen Amen Amen

That We May Realize

The demons seek to control us
With their horror and their greed
They seek to spread their darkness
To fulfill their unholy needs

God has given His children
A gift beyond belief
The freedom to make choices
From darkness, there is relief

This freedom we use daily
In all we say and do
But do we really ponder
On the paths that we ensue

God, help us with our choices
That they may be Heaven blessed
That we may realize our Holiness
To rise above the rest

Amen Amen Amen

Coming Home

Always

Always and forever
My Presence to you is near
Call out to the Heavens
Ask My Voice, to hear

Always and forever
Are the Promises I make
Listen for My guidance
Listen for Life's sake

Always and forever
Eternity be told
Pray to the Father, Son and Spirit
Heaven to behold

Always and forever
Is the Father's Love
Listen to the Angels sing
The Holy Songs from above

Amen Amen Amen

Faith Is The Answer

I will not leave you desolate
I will come when you call
With Blessings from the Father
The Savior, the All

You will see me forever
If you believe
My Promise eternal
You, I will not leave

Let not your hearts be troubled
Let not your souls grieve
In my Father's House are many rooms
For those who believe

The Promises of Heaven
Are for His children to seek
The young and the old
The strong and the weak

Faith is the Answer
Love is the Call
God is eternal
For one and for all

Amen Amen Amen

Call To Worship

Man has so many celebrations
To glorify themselves
To bask in their accomplishments
A job they do so well

God in all Your Splendor
It is time to give You praise
For giving us life
For our Blessings all our days

God in Your Holiness
It is time for Your Honor
Praises be sung
There is no other

God in the stillness
Let us hear Your Voice
Let us adorn You
Let You be our choice

Let man not be so blinded
By the obscurities at hand
That they fail to worship
The Father who created man

Man creates the boundaries
And the demons they give homage to
Let us not forget
All Honor belongs to You

Amen Amen Amen

The Eastern Light Did Raise

Our shame was cleansed with His Blood
Our sins were washed away
All Glory to the Father
Our world is healed today

Easter is upon us
A day of Holy Praise
The Father sent the Son
The Eastern Light did raise

Jesus, You taught us
With Your actions and Your ways
With Your Voice and with Your Miracles
That God is with us all our days

All Glory to the Father
All Honor and all Praise
The Father sent the Son
The Eastern Light did raise

Father You stood before us
As we are unholy and unclean
Father You forgave us
Eternal Love is seen

All Glory to the Father
Our voices raised in Praise
The Father sent the Son
The Eastern Light did raise

Amen Amen Amen

You Are Not Alone

The journey is overwhelming
The tests more than some can bear
But I will walk with you always
If you call My Presence there

You will not be alone
Nor forgotten in this life
Call out My Name
I will ease your burden of strife

I am always near you
It is you who shuts the door
Call out to the Heavens
That your soul may eternally soar

Amen Amen Amen

His Footsteps Are Before Us

His footsteps we would follow
Would emulate His life
To teach man how to conquer
The darkness and the strife

What lessons did Jesus teach us
Look closely and you will see
He gave us all the answers
To a better life and to Thee

He came in the form of a human
And taught us in many ways
Reflect upon His words
And His actions, in His days

He showed us we could conquer
Darkness in every form
And transcend the boundaries
The human condition calls the norm

Jesus preformed miracles
And Faith could conquer still
The obstacles of this world
Even the darkest will

His footsteps are before us
It is our choice to make
To follow in His Will
The chains of death to break

Amen Amen Amen

Shelter Beneath His Wings

You will find shelter beneath His Wings
You will be protected from the storm
You will know the Love of Heaven
If you call upon the Lord

I will Shelter all my Children
Even in the darkest days
I will carry them above the chaos
When they choose to follow my Ways

My Love is eternal
As the Father is the Son
The Spirit is enduring
The Love of Heaven, One

I will stand before you
I will take your pain
Call to Me as your Father
All of Heaven to gain

You will find shelter beneath His Wings
You will be protected from the storm
You will know the Love of Heaven
If you call upon the Lord

Amen Amen Amen

I Will Stand Before You
I Will Take Your Pain
Call To Me As Your Father
All Of Heaven To Gain
Amen
Amen
Amen

www.ingramcontent.com/pod-product-compliance
Lightning Source LLC
Chambersburg PA
CBHW051711040426
42446CB00008B/833